A is for AFRICA

Written by Michael I. Samulak
Illustrated by Sswaga Sendiba

www.trafford.com

North America & international
toll-free: 1 888 232 4444 (USA & Canada)
phone: 250 383 6864 ♦ fax: 250 383 6804
email: info@trafford.com

The United Kingdom & Europe
phone: +44 (0)1865 722 113 ♦ local rate: 0845 230 9601
facsimile: +44 (0)1865 722 868 ♦ email: info.uk@trafford.com

10 9 8 7 6 5 4 3

For my son Joshua, love Daddy.

A is for Africa.

Africa is an awesome land, as we soon shall see. It is home to many amazing animals, people, and trees.

B is for baboon.

The baboon has an energy that is playful, but tough. Don't cross his path or things could get rough.

C is for cheetah.

"Swift as a cheetah," so it is said
both near and far.
Running at top speed, these cats
can keep up with your car!

D is for drum.

The drum is an instrument of choice whose rhythm and beat make the people rejoice!

E is for elephant.

The elephant moves steady and slow. Together in herds they often go.

F is for fowl.

The many fabulous fowl that fill the African sky can hardly be matched by other birds nearby.

G is for giraffe.

The giraffe is the gentle giant of the land. She stands head and shoulders above every animal or man.

H is for hippopotamus.

The hippo on land is surprisingly so at ease. They are equally at home in the rivers or sea.

I is for ibis.

The ibis, a bird with a long slender beak, searches and probes for a nice tasty treat!

J is for jars.

The jars of earth and wood made here are impressive indeed, and yet so useful for every-day needs.

K is for kob.

The kob is a kind of African antelope. It spends its time grazing in fields, or bounding about on a hill or a slope.

L is for lion.

The lion surveys the land with heart-filled pride. This king of beasts wields a mighty roar and has a piercing eye.

M is for mountain gorilla.

The mountain gorilla is quite simply magnificent — loving, strong, and highly intelligent.

N is for Nile crocodile.

The Nile crocodile is mysterious, silent, and sleek. In the river he lies, without making a peep.

O is for ostrich.

The ostrich is known for her long neck and strong legs. She also is famous for laying large eggs.

P is for pygmy chimpanzee.

The pygmy chimpanzee's face reveals a soul that is caring, imaginative, and ever so thoughtful.

Q is for queen.

The queen of the village is the oldest woman who is gentle as a dove. She is adorned with all wisdom and always acts in love.

Ris for rhinoceros.

The rhino's horn is beautiful, long, and white. It forever displays courage and strength to foe and friend alike.

S is for spotted hyena.

The spotted hyena live together in groups called clans. They hunt in packs, or simply wait, to clean up after others in the land.

T is for tilapia.

The tilapia fish a prize catch does make for all those hard at work on the rivers and lakes.

U is for Uganda's crowned crane.

This crane is a national symbol of Uganda, *"The Pearl"*. Their feathers adorn the crowns of kings and the heads of young girls.

V is for village.

The village is where you will find many people of the land. Here they are happy to lend each other a helping hand.

W is for warthog.

The warthog can easily be found rumbling around through tall grass or the dust of dry ground.

X is for Xolani.
Xolani, Saba, Nadijah, and Muata are just some of their names.

Like you and me they love to laugh with friends, and play lots of games!

Y is for yellow mongoose.

The yellow mongoose makes a most curious sound. It walks with a wiggle and stays close to the ground.

Z is for zebra.

The zebra's stripes help keep him safe, as you may know. Even so, they are still careful and always stay on their toes.

THE END